AMBUSH

To Ed Jones, a fondly
remembered crewmate
aboard the USS Sirago (SS485)
and a cherished friend.

Harold Webster
January 11, 2002

Ambush

and Other Poems

by

Harold S. Webster

Illustrations
by
Joan Henrik

ISBN 0-615-11947-6

My friends and family have urged me to publish these few poems, and I have consistently resisted the idea, realizing there is no great demand even for the masterworks of Robert Frost and Walt Whitman. However, I was finally persuaded to publish a few copies in book form, just to see how far they might go.

Since you, the reader, now have the book in hand, I trust you will soon begin reading it, and I want to start you off with a warning: I am fond of rhythm and rhyme, but I don't always put the rhyme where the reader expects it. I do not capitalize the initial letter in each line. I believe that old convention serves mainly as an impediment to smooth reading.

I further believe that writing a poem is basically an act of subversion. A verse that coincides with thoughts generally agreed upon is no poem. It is, rather, a sentiment, like the gentle musings on a greeting card. Most good poems, it seems to me, are seasoned with a little vinegar and salt. They take a crack at things as they are and suggest in one way or another that whatever is, isn't quite as it should be.

And so, with that dangerous thought in my head, I began some long time ago to write what passes muster with me as poetry. I wanted my verses to make sense, but I also wanted to tug a little at the brain, to maybe cause a little consternation or discomfort.

I also hope you find something here that pleases your senses. Read on.

Harold S. Webster
August 2001

Ambush

and Other Poems

To my wife Kay and our children,
Paul and Rachael.

H. W.

Ambush

The poem slinks
like a stalking cat
catches us rapt in rhythms,
unsuspecting,
like a bird pecking on a suet ball,
then bites us in the throat,
slays solace with a slash
of fang-sharp thought
that stuns one's senses,
jagged dissonance,
torn tin
a tart surprise
like tomato slices on the thighs.

The Monarch

We both had caught our butterflies
and in a green glade
we spread their wings
and looked them over
in dappled light.
Billy's was of course
the larger and opaque
but mine had something silver in it
and so I said,
"Look at mine, Billy,
look at mine."

He would not see my butterfly.

He turned his eyes upon his own
and lost himself in orange
and black.

What I Would Have Said

I thought of something sharp to say today,
a clever barb that would exemplify my class
and make me certain champion of the fray
and a great perfect fool of the arrogant ass
I fussed with; but sad to say it came too late.
My adversary long since had left the scene,
content at having flogged me in debate.
Damn him then, I'll never be serene
again until I can renew the quarrel
and verbally skewer this smug-ugly twit
with an elegant thrust of my rapier-like wit...
but, wait ... I cannot deliver my practiced snarl,
because ... God help me ... I've forgotten the thought;
I fret in cold fury but revenge comes to naught.

Money

luscious stuff
passport to paradise
icon of never enough,
stay with me;
melt my lover's ice
chase away my hungers
clad me nice
draw friends to me
and jolly pleasures
to suffice
in lieu of love,
rid me of burdens drear
cloak me in respect
and most of all
make me seem sincere

■

Time

He works slick
like snot on a doorknob
filching
from us as we
gaze away,
a muscle cell or two
and now and then a bit of bone,
surgery sans pain
with negative gain.

He takes the tawny hairs
and slips in white ones;
makes the knees ache,
scribes tiny lines
around the eyes
and spreads incontinence
across the continents;
enough's enough, I say.
I aim to catch him at it
yet today
and put him away;
I'll pummel him
and humble him,
make him suffer
as we do
until he's past recidivism;
threats will not distract me,
nor criticism.
No grave matters
can shake
me from my quest;
I will stay awake tonight
 I will not rest
nor sleep here ever again
until he's caught.
At least I ought.

Line Fences

It was idle talk about line fences
that seemed to set her off.
Raining hard it was, so all hands
came to wait it out;
  some whittled sticks
  and others talked as if quite well informed
about how long good locust posts might last
compared with old used crossties.

Then Rachel stopped rocking
and spoke in raspy voice,
pointing yonder off a ways as if
she'd seen a bad thing and wished
to make it stop:
"It stood right there," she said,
"an oak tree, old and odd it was,
and shivered more'n once by lightning.

"I miss it so.
While back they lopped it down
to run a new line fence.
I say it made no sense.
You need old things like that
to tell you where you're at."

And Rachel rocked in the tall chair.
The hands stopped jawing for a spell
then spoke in quieter tones of crops.

Something to Fret About

From fuzzy far galaxies, many a night,
someone discovers faint sprays of light
that started toward us eons in the past.

But now that the starlight has reached us ,
little, I think, it can teach us,
now that we see it at last.

What if alien forms had sent us
some godawful fright with that light?
Suppose we should find that at a far time
terrible things were pending:
like wars about petroleum
the banning of linoleum
the preeminence of jocks
rules in schools against wearing no socks
inflation-driven spending
a bull market's ending,
perhaps a great famine on a faraway planet?

O damn it! O frustrating sonofagun!
Even, by chance, if we got there right now
we could not change what's long ago done,
nor even be helpful by showing them how;
(Too bad, such advice can lighten a brow.)

But just to further befuddle the fuss,
would it not seem, anyhow, preposterous
to be hearing such stuff from the likes of us?

Old Men Sitting on the Front Porch Fussing

They sat alone on the front porch fussing,
as two old men are often apt to do,
on what the modern world was coming to;
not exactly wasting time discussing
things, but more like helping time along.
Willard was the oldest, by a year or two,
enough, he thought, to show most others wrong.
But truth be told they both were near the end.
Willard was a worn-out dairy farmer
with arthritic hands that now would hardly bend,
and Otis, with wizened skin like old cracked armor
had been a teacher at the local school.
Neither had another living friend.
Neither was, by all accounts, a fool.

"Otis, I s'pose you don't know how work was
some long time back, you being pretty much exempt,
so you'd not remember much of Emil Hahn.
And my guess'd be you never would attempt
to do what he could do before the dawn."

"They said hard work wouldn't do me any harm
but I declined to risk it. So what's this old Hahn done?"
Otis asked.

   "I'm talking 'bout some hellish warm
work constructing proper haystacks on the farm;
it was a vital skill that few could do,
at least not right, I don't mind telling you."

"And who on earth would think he'd even want to?"
Otis asked. "And anyhow there's more to work
than muscle. You really never had a clue
about brainwork; you thought it simply meant to shirk;
but press on, Willard, you're bustin' to review
what it was this Emil Hahn could do
and I'll not keep you from it, go ahead." >

"Well, you know, how haying then got done.
We did it most with pitchforks. Used to dread
the sweat and dust and white-hot blistering sun.
Hardly ever saw a baler or a combine.
We'd hitch the horses up to rake and tedder
and fling the hay to dry in windrow long lines,
bunch it up in shocks, then hell-for-leather
drag the shocks off to the stack and pitch
the hay to Emil, and watch him weave it,
fork by fork, like placing cloth to stitch."

Here Willard paused a spell as if he'd leave it
there and choose instead the thought to savor
and not encumber brain with task of talk.

But Otis noticed soon and said, "Why'd you balk
for heaven's sake? For once you'd kept me half awake.
Now you've begun, get on with it and favor
me with all this lore about your Emil Hahn."

Willard looked as if his train had gone
but caught himself and then continued on:
"Yes we'd watch him weave each separate swatch,
lock one upon the other in ever tighter rounds
and coax it all together slowly into a slope
and well-nigh perfect geometric cone,
then slide by rope off to the stubbled ground.
His stacks shed rain and guarded hay from heat
and kept the good alfalfa clean and sweet.
Old Emil then was always in demand
We paid him well to keep him here on hand."

"So whatever is the use of that, I say.
Could Emil even find a job today?
Today we need no cones nor long condone
slow ways like that to reap the county's bounty."   >

"Now that's the very point I think I've shown.
The time is gone today for Emil Hahn
just like for you and me in Laurel County.
I'll bet a dollar, too, you couldn't teach
today, the way you must've taught back then."

Otis didn't answer right away.
His face looked withered now and gray.
Willard waited for a friend to have his say.

"Oh yes, I'd somehow manage now to reach
again the kids today. Don't want to anyway.
I'm too ornery now for classroom action
and not apt to act to parents' satisfaction,
but, by God, I still could do it well.

"I'm different from your old hay stacker friend
He had no other skill to tell or sell
and the coming of the baler spelled his end."

"We're just exactly like him, both of us.
We're useless, don't you know, like shaley rust.
You want to know what finally made him go?"

"No, but I expect I'm gonna hear it anyway,
so do your worst, make it short and fire away."

"He came again that May, I think it was a Saturday
and sat here looking nervous on our stoop
and asked my mother where he'd find my dad.
She said, 'Why Emil, he's baling on the slope;
won't you come in and have a bowl of soup?
It's really good though not the best we've had.
I think it's over salted,' or some such thing, she said.
You know how mother always carried on. >

"She filled a bowl and called again to him;
she says she filled it to the very brim
and called and called but he'd already gone.

"Where he went we never figured out.
Some say they saw him bucking bales somewhere.
Too bad, if true, he had a talent rare.
I'd guess he wasn't good at that nor stout
enough to last the season's haying through.
But still he wouldn't quit, I'm telling you.
Hurt he was but still a trooper true."

▓

Sylvan Rhapsody

Chauncy Stubbs, the large nymph,
flits heavily among sere hyacinths
and jaded jonquils,
swerves coyly in diaphanous,
manufactured gowns,
calling out in dulcet tones for
his homely paramour,
and all the while the lush reek of thick toes
hangs warmly in the fetid air.

Comes Juanita now, the buxom troll,
gliding through silken mud
in equally radiant raiment
toward her fumbling love.

They touch, perform pliés,
and sing a silver lay
of healing wounds
and ancient spoons
and lovely tubs of brie.

And all the while,
deep in the dark, enchanted woods,
their feet make strange echoes.

▪

Christmas

An onus on us,
a wrestling with nettles,
irksome extras we've no time for,
eyes glazed over in a raucous mall,
daze of spending,
beglittering a tree,
wrapping boxes, baking cookies, making fudge
hanging great pungent wreaths
and draping long strings of glowing light
from eaves, and blue-spruce trees,
like captive fireworks
frozen in mid-bang.

Christ, when's it all to end?

If it weren't for spicy smells
cozy old melodies that make us cry
good warm cookies
egg nog, Tom 'n Jerrys,
mothers and fathers
brothers and sisters
cousins and uncles
and the cold crisp air
and the friendliness
and big hugs
and kids squealing with delight
and good cheer everywhere,

We wouldn't bother, would we.

On Raising a Child

Raising a child, I'll say if you ask,
is a heavy load, a right tough task;
mostly a matter, I'll probably say,
of wondering just what to do,
and then, after thinking it thoroughly through
and pausing some seconds to pray,
you still end up, quite matter of factly,
doing or saying the wrong thing exactly;

I marvel that kids can ever survive
these assaults on their lives
and grow up as folks we can trust.
It's somewhat unsettling
despite all our meddling
they still turn out better than us.

※

The Tunnel at Red River Gorge
and the Boy who Died There

We drove down a narrow road,
itself a gash in solid rock
with giant ranks of hemlock,
hickory, beech, oak and maple
hemming us in,
rising high to dim the sun
and then, sudden-like,
a great wall of tan sandstone
rose to block the road
and we had to stop,
get out of the car
and look straight up to see
the top.

And then we turned our eyes
upon the dark tunnel
looking small in the base of massive stone
chopped crudely in
like a jagged stab wound.

And we read about how the tunnel
came to be and the good old boy*
who died there
thawing sticks of frozen dynamite
beside a fire.

Somebody told that boy to do this thing
we thought.
Somebody said "Go warm this up,"
and the simple boy complied
and died for his obedience.

░

*His name was Charles McNab, a lad who claimed to be 17
and had no prior experience with explosives.*

My Computer

hideous tumor of plastic and wire
your incredible growth is insidious,
your presence alarming, invidious,
your ill-timed crashes perfidious
and yet, what's so maddingly piteous,
you're obviously undowithoutidious.

✳

Sleep

Something solemn sleeping is,
an old ritual done slow and slow,
a druid trance that for a time
frees us from the tyranny of mind
and its frantic, frenzied dance;
it keeps the burdens briefly from us
so cells and cells can cleanse themselves
and lets us rise with clear eyes
refreshed, keen
and new like dew on clover;

But something thrives
that won't abide such torpor;
it strives and strives to penetrate
the sweet deep languor
and lure us in
to cogitate great knots again.
It is the shrill cacophony of day,
a toneless song that will not pass,
a bad tenor in an endless mass.

※

Slants

Let us now be honest:
all things bend from plumb.
Nothing straight persists.
Telephone poles sunk in tundra
lean way over
and yarrow yields with the wind,
and so do oaks and timothy stalks;
and lines of chalk
if they run long enough
will circle the earth for eternity.

Light in the sky that hits my eye
from somebody else's galaxy
has bent all to hell to get here as well.

So, is honesty, too, a fallacy?

Ode to Lonnie Edwards

Where did you get that curious streak,
that charming delivery
whenever you speak?

You got it from the Laurel County hills
where the mountain folk sing
the songs that cause chills
and sweet rhythms fill
the air like silver-soft wings.

It was, also, I think, a gift inherent,
a very special gift from good Kentucky parents.

And where did you get that knack for neat
tricks,
that odd way of getting those asinine
kicks?

I well know the answer to that one, dadburnit,
I was there when you first, by god, came to
learn it.

I know that your folks
from early on saw to it
that you'd learn practical jokes
and how to put victims through it.

They had an old gray Ford,
a thirty-six, as I recall,
a thirty-six with running boards,
where you victimized both me and Paul!

It was a two-door job with mohair seats
and windows that wouldn't roll down;
they'd park it in sun to gather up heat >

enough to charbroil a good cut of meat
and then they'd take off into town
with me and Paul and you, the clown,
in the back of that old Ford.

You'd sit between us, all nice and neat,
as off to a somewhere we roared
and always your daddy, just to be sweet,
would buy you a double-dip ice cream cone
treat.

We'd travel along in the heat
and dead air, and dreading the time
(cause we knew it was coming),
when drowsed by tires humming
you'd fall sound asleep and daub
us with slime.

We couldn't, of course, condone
the curse of the cone
but these were inexorable things;
sometimes we dodged your thrusts and your
flings and we did it with consummate skill
but you'd always recover
and try for another
and finally come in for the kill.

We'd piss and moan
but you slept like a stone
and no matter how valiant our will,
you'd always end up as clean as a bone
and we'd end up wearing the cone.

And sometimes when I'm trying real hard
and I'm having a good run o' luck 'll
see once again that wheezy old Ford,
and still hear your dad's quiet chuckle.

Death of a Dog

Our dog Tommy died today.
He will no longer drool on anybody
nor leave a fuzz of hair on furniture
nor sleep in the forbidden chair
nor lick himself when visitors are here
nor eat cat food behind our backs.
In fact he will do none of that.
So why it is we miss him so?
I think I know: he loved us true
and forgave us gladly our faults, too.

Slowing

My mind takes me where I no longer prowl,
and like an old dog who sleeps while chasing prey,
who flicks his paws and makes a muted howl,
I sometimes see me late on a cold day
trekking near Tok,* or some such place,
in knee-deep snow with a stiff gale
blowing sleet into my bearded face;
There's danger here, for if in darkness I should fail
to reach my cabin, nestled in the woods a ways,
I would never live to tell this dream;
they'd find me in the thaw of warmer days
with open eyes beside a flowing stream.
I see me slowing in the blowing snow,
It is, I think, a lovely way to go.

▓

* Tok: a small town in southeastern Alaska on the south shore of
the Tanana River and near the Canadian border.

43

Silver Song

My son will play his horn for me
although I will not ask him to.

But pretty soon he'll
lift that horn
and make the air seem silvery
and set the leaves aquiver,
playing maybe Amazing Grace
the Navy Hymn
or Taps.

And then will come a time of quiet.

Jump Shot

the clock stopped
just before he got the shot off
but we held our breaths anyway
as if this once it wasn't so,
made it all go dead quiet
and watched the ball
arc outrageously high
and swoosh unhindered through the hoop,
a lovely shot anyhow
all the prettier perhaps
because it came too late.

I see him now
arm still and forever extended
wrist cocked
fingers spread
a classic pose frozen
in my mind.

He didn't know the game was over.
He'd carved perfection in the air.
The end came unexpected
and took hm unaware.

■

The Visitor

I saw him as he walked away
and thought he was kinfolk,
maybe an uncle,
in clean bib overalls,
Oshkoshers,
brogans,
faded flannel shirt with
buttoned-up collar and sleeves
and a snap-bill leather cap
like farmers back home once wore;
he was walking out the door,
the glass door at the end of the hall
and a far trek from
where I'd been.
I thought I heard somebody whisper,
"That's The Visitor.
He stood there while you slept."

And then he stopped and looked back at me,
and I hobbled to him pulling my intravenous
trolley with me, and I said,
"Sorry about being asleep,
just wanted to see your face."
He looked kindly, I thought, but didn't say so.
What I said was,
"You look like someone I know."

He nodded, smiled easy like,
and answered the unasked: "Yes," he said,
"but you've still got things to do.
I'll come again another time."

Then he touched his cap bill, smiled again
and walked away.

▩

Snow

Do you know snow,
the kind that hangs in air like smoke
and makes near woods seem far away,
a vapor veil, translucent gray;
a snow so dry it will not pack
in balls for kids to fling?
If you know snow at all
then tell me why this thing of wind
spins to drifts in tire ruts
piles up high behind fence rails,
tool sheds, huts,
and all things standing tall.

I know snow.

I know why.

Snow does not like
to be in sky
It glides behind things thick and thin
so it can quietly settle in
and spread in drifts like flakes of down
and rest from constant swirling
round.

The Danger of Paper

Paper hurts in many ways:
If they pile it on you deep enough
it can crush your chest
so be very careful with it,
I suggest.

It has sharp edges, too,
and sometimes cuts one's thumbs
I've heard that some cuts never heal
and that the victim, like as not, succumbs.

It's mostly hurtful though with ink upon it
and morbid words that make you feel despondent.

Or blabberings that waste your time
or, as the case is here,
with aimless rhyme.

Confession

Have you as I have said you'd do
something that you did not do?
Did chores pile up to fill your cup
or did you simply drop the knot,
and let the rope slide through?
How does it make you feel, you heel?

Sources

All things come from other things
like rain from cloud,
oak from acorn
flower from seed
like grass from sod
like iron from ore
like us, by lore, from God

We know this here is true
or think we do
We trace all things to source
of course
which is what God wants us to.

But still we curious want to know,
can the answer ever come.
Will we ever know for sure, we ask,
where God Herself came from?

Oh, ever still the thought remains
that strains our simple brains:
could something ever always be?
If not, why not? say we.

What's the ultimate source of all
and what gave birth to it?
I'd like to know true fact on that
and have the pope dispute it.

Unbuilding a Good God

We built ourselves a god one day,
this time a really nice one
who helped us out a lot
and never hurt us
and never let bad things occur
like holocausts and bloody war
and never made us worship her
and never did get mad at us
whenever we would err.

Our god for certain loved us truly
although, we now suspect, unduly,
because one day some awful things occurred
and we are verifiably perturbed:
Somebody saw our god was made of clay
and noticed bad things happened anyway
somebody sinned
the roof fell in
somebody lied
the old clay dried
the good god died
our prayers abruptly curbed

Who's to blame
let's say the name
it's one we cannot trust
It's neither god nor Jim nor Jill
it's every one of us.

▓

Demise of Wee Glintings

I thought I saw moonflecks
flickering on a lazy lake,
but maybe moon they weren't;
I think they may have been the glintings,
wee bright beings
rising for air like fireworks from a deep place
only to drown in windchop.
And perhaps the music of the waves
on this too cool night
was really glintings' wails.
I do not know for sure.
I tried to scoop them for a better look
and bring them in to shore
but they slipped the seine
and died before my eyes
and I could do no more.

Death of a Horsefly

the stuttered buzz was cut
and the thumb-wide fly
swooped onto sweat flecks
on the roan stud,
and sucked blood,
but Billy, the kind kid,
scooped it up quick
and thrust a slender timothy stalk into its guts
and tossed the so-stuck fly
upward into sun.

To watch a spiraling fly die
is thrilling stuff for kind kids
and roan studs.

It has to do with point of view.

▩

Death of a Woodchuck

We watched the farmer kill the mad woodchuck.
At least he told us it was mad.
We stood in silence while he thumped its head
till it was bloody, still and dead
Too bad we thought
the furry thing seemed friendly:
waddled right up to us,
sat pertly on his haunches
as if to say "I'll have a handout now."

He did not cry nor shield himself from harm
and I wondered then what prompted all the fuss.
I should have thought the farm was big enough
for him and us.

Could we have kept the critter in a cage,
I asked, and watched him closely for a spell?
Did we really need to kill him off
so quickly like a beast from bloody hell?

He merely turned and looked at me impatiently.
And would not answer straight. He only said,
"He acted strange. You should be glad he's dead."

I saw the common sense of what he said
but also knew I never could be glad.

The Watcher

A great black bird-thing sits hunched up
atop a locust post just out of sight
behind me ever watching.
I sometimes almost see it in periphery
but never quite.

The Thundermug

Buford de Lesips, long since plumb dead,
went one cold night to his corn shuck bed
with a thought in his head
that being alone in his cabin
was close to heaven
as he'd likely get,
safe from cold wind and the clatter of sleet
all tucked in on a warm flannel sheet,
thick thermal socks upon his feet
and buried in blankets of wool.
And no one around to bully and pull
him and make him do hard chores and all.

But now and again, sometimes on a whim
but mostly to answer the call,
quivering and shivering
he'd rise up to pee, though he barely could see
and judged only by sound
if his urine had found
that quaint old jug, the old Thundermug,
that porceline pot
every family had got,
and the very thing he claimed
that he aimed for,
though not quite successfully.

Shivering stressfully,
he stood in the cold,
his manhood on hold
till the very last dribble had left him,
and started for bed but came back instead
to the place where his urine bereft him,

for he had no choice, he'd heard that voice
the voice, he afterwards said,
of his long dead dad
who raved from the grave: >

"Now, Buford, you shiftless young sot,
are you still lazy or have you forgot
  the last one to use it must empty the pot.
Don't leave it, you deviant, to molder and stink
You're old enough now to be able to think!

"You've been told, no matter the cold,
you've been told and, by Christ, you should know it,
to wipe up the floor, walk out the door
and find a good place you can throw it!"

Windblown Cloud at Sunset

I saw a ship of shaded pearl
plowing an azure sky
and watched her flags of cream unfurl
before my practiced eye.

Her silver sails soon billowed out
and caught the wind to run
and on she hurled
above the world
to fight the blazing sun

The battle raged
Old Sol engaged
and tinged her canvas, too
The good ship blazed
a white flag raised,
she sank in endless blue.

Hurts

pain uncoils from deep within,
spreading chill like a winter storm attack,
or sometimes like a thin icepick
that stabs the muscles of the back

sometimes a neon line appears before the eyes —
a zigzag wire that flicks and shimmers —
and a great fist grips inside the skull
and causes focus tremors

but we are old, inured to small distress
and try to take all inner hurts in stride;
to stand erect and do what must be done,
and never yield to private aches inside.

■

The Butternut Boys

Hurrah again for the butternut boys
who fought for the CSA.
How gallant they seem
with the passage of time,
how grand the old generals in gray.

But the boys, the boys,
they died in furious battle
amid smoke, and screams
and sharp musket rattle
for a cause they well understood;
and it wasn't the right to own manhood
nor preserve the life they knew.

For the life they led for all but a few
was being dirt poor and ill fed.
Most never thought of owning a slave
just mostly of getting ahead.

Oh certain they knew what they fought for,
the same reason all soldiers say;
they fought for the right to keep living
to breathe for another today.

Nobody died for the Stars and Bars,
no more than they died for Old Glory.
Both sides vied to save their own hides,
and that's all there is to the story.

The Last Refuge

A man totes the flag on his arm.
He thinks it will keep him from harm.
When anyone questions,
or makes good suggestions,
he waves it aloft in alarm.

To muffle the sound of passed gas
he toots on a horn made of brass;
he frequently mentions
his noble intentions
and tattoos the flag on his ass.

Song of the Gandy Dancers

If you'd a got drunk
you'd a been okay
working on a chain gang
for a sight better pay
Whoom

All together now
gotta lift that rail
when the boss say heave it, boys,
ya better do not fail
Move

Set that bar, boys,
lift that tie
shovel them rocks in
it's do-by-god or die.
All together, now boys,
this I tell
grab that bar 'n give 'er Willy hell
Move

Lift that crosstie,
tamp that rock
don't you worry none 'bout that clock
Chugga Chug Chug

Mama's got grits 'n collard greens
best damn cookin' that ya ever seen
Whoom

■

The Last Stand
A Prelude

They came easy-loping over the rise
flags flying,
leather creaking on the hoofbeat,
a double line of blue-clad boys
in sinuous files
like twin gliding snakes
till Custer spotted dust
and saw a few braves
skedaddlng,
more 'n likely
fleeing the wrath
of the mighty goddam 7th Cavalry
and the long-haired
fearless fighter
commanding...
"After 'em boys,
make 'em howl"....

■

Custer
The Epilogue

Oglalla Two-Kettle, Hunkpapa, too,
Sitting Bull, Red Cloud, Crazy Horse
Lakota bloody Sioux.
Dust, blood, screams,
bullets, arrows swirling,
painted ponies all awhirling,
howls at shrieking decibel.
It was a slaughter-awful scene
a scene from bloody-cluttered hell.

And there within the whirling spot
beleaguered blue boys dropped,
and the green-gold grass grew red
with counting coup, and killing, too,
and Yellowhair dead.

And all around that night
the Indian camp stood mute
There was no joy, no victory dance
the only sound a flute.

■

On Useless Things

Do you now hear the great clock click
that tells you soon the warming sun will set,
and knowing that your day is dying quick
do your work a little faster and forget
as best you can the dimming of the light,
like a sparrow in a fret to build its nest
races with the dusk and dark of night?
Let me in friendship quietly suggest
a lighter load for you to tow instead,
although I too have tremors in my chest
and terrors plenty in my graying head:
Slow down, I say, go do some useless thing,
like pet a pup or hear some children sing.

To Kay

When I consider how my life was spent
and all the other things I might have done,
I find I have but little to repent.
In fact, I'd say, it comes to mostly none.
Except I should have been a better mate;
and been more kind and caring of your feelings.
I'm sorry now, I know that thought comes late
so please forgive my distance and odd dealings.
But yet I think our balance beam was true:
We smoothed most chafes with grace and quiet calm.
We fussed a bit as all good couples do
but soothed the deepest hurts with healing balm.
Although at times we seemed to live apart,
I know I've loved you in my deepest heart.

About the Author

Harold S. Webster was born and raised in
rural northern Kentucky where he experienced
both the gladness and sadness that characterize
much of his poetry. He has had his fill of hard,
low-tech farmwork. He has worked as a bridge
painter on the old L&N Railroad, as a hod carrier
for brick masons, and as a driver of a tractor-trailer
rig hauling hogs from Peoria to King of Prussia,
Pennsylvania. In the 1950s he was an electronics
technician in the US Navy submarine service.
He was educated at Wartburg College and the
University of Minnesota and taught English in
Iowa and Minnesota high schools. His career
includes executive level experiences as a public
relations professional for corporations and
communications firms. He is now semi-retired
as the former owner and now chairman of an
advertising company in Duluth, Minnesota.
He and his wife Kay live near Carlton, Minnesota
on a quiet 15-acre retreat with a 30-year-old horse,
four neurotic cats and one black dog.